MW01618668
Little Kicker
Country
where we live
Tony the Pony's
clover patch
Farmer John's
barn
Emma Cow's mountain path
Watercress Patch
Sandy the Sow
Pig's mud hole
Daddy & Mother
Donkey's grazing
spot
Little Kicker's
kicking circle

Written and
illustrated by
Sandy
Sprott
Little
Kicker's
First Rainstorm

Little Kicker's
First Rainstorm

This

Little Kicker Book

is presented to

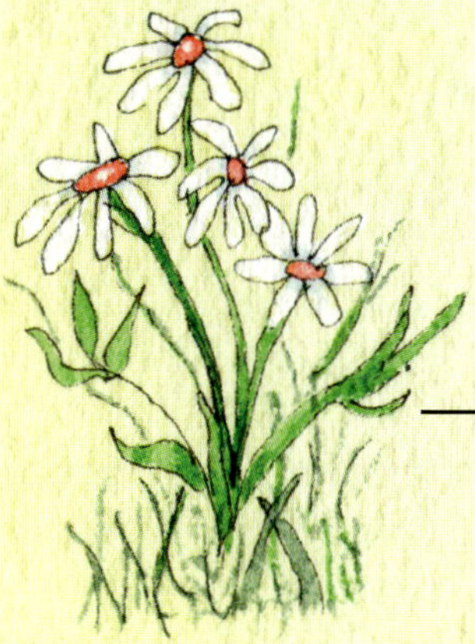

NAME

by

NAME OF RELATIVE, FRIEND, CHURCH OR ORGANIZATION

OCCASION DATE

Little Kicker's First Rainstorm

Published by Kimble Creek Press LLC, Hermitage, Missouri
Cover and text design by Diane King, dkingdesigner.com
Editing by Sam Sprott

Publisher's Cataloging-in-Publication data
Sprott, Sandy.
Little Kicker's first rainstorm / Sandy Sprott.
p. cm.
ISBN: 978-0-9843956-2-0 (Hardcover)
ISBN: 978-0-9843956-3-7 (pbk.)
Summary: Little Kicker, a donkey, learns that rain is important
and prayer can help him get over his fears.

[1. Rain and rainfall--Fiction. 2. Donkeys --Fiction. 3. Prayer --Fiction.] I. Title.

PZ7.S7688 Li 2012

[E] --dc23 2012903382

Manufactured by Color House Graphics, Inc., Grand Rapids, MI, USA
Second Printing, March 2014
Job # 41970
www.LittleKicker.com

MADE IN U.S.A.

This book is dedicated to our son, Tony. Your humor and enjoyment of life continue to energize and encourage your father and me. You have always loved racing, thus, in this series of books about Little Kicker and his friends, you are Tony the Pony, the fastest thing on four hoofs. You are a faithful friend to Little Kicker, and your Dad and I love you beyond the rim of time. Enjoy!

Little Kicker is a newborn donkey colt. He lives on a farm with other friendly animals.

"Croooak," said Mr. Frog.

"Where are you going?" asked Little Kicker.

"I am going to my home in the pond," replied Mr. Frog as he went hop and plop, hop and plop!

Big, dark clouds floated in front of the sun.

Mr. Frog jumped into his home in the pond.

"Baroom, Aroom, Oom!"

Thunder boomed from the sky.

Little Kicker screamed with fear! "Hee Haw, Hee Haw!"

"Hee Haaaw," Mother Donkey answered as she ran to Little Kicker.

Mother Donkey said, “Don’t be afraid. Look, it is starting to rain.”

But Little Kicker did not like the rain. He jumped up on his back legs.

Little Kicker wanted to run away from the rain, but still stay close to Mother Donkey.

Little Kicker kicked to the left.

He kicked to the middle.

He kicked to the right.

Little Kicker tried to
kick the raindrops away.

Mother Donkey ran to Little Kicker. He hid his face under her neck. “Now, now,” said Mother Donkey, “the rain is good for us.”

She gently rubbed his head and wrapped her tail around him, holding him close.

Daddy Donkey came running. He wanted to make sure that Little Kicker was okay. Daddy wanted to teach Little Kicker to pray when he is afraid.

Daddy Donkey, Mother Donkey and
Little Kicker prayed for God
to keep them safe.

Little Kicker asked, “Why does it rain?”

Daddy Donkey answered, “God sends rain so we have water to drink. See this yummy grass? We love to eat it. The grass must have water to grow. The trees give us shade. Trees need a lot of water. God sends rain because he loves us.”

Little Kicker wanted to be brave. He stepped away from Daddy and Mother Donkey.

Just when he took a bite of grass…

Thunder boomed loudly across the sky.
BAROOM, AROOM, OOM!

Little Kicker jumped in fear.

Little Kicker remembered that he should not be afraid. God would help him. "I wonder," he thought, "is God helping my friends?" Little Kicker looked at Rachael.

Rachael the Little Red Hen was not afraid of the rain and thunder. She was smiling as she fluffed up her pretty, red feathers. Rachael was thankful for a bath.

Tony the Pony was not afraid. He played in the rain by running circles around Sam the Lamb. "I love eating wet grass," said Sam the Lamb. "Um! Um!"

Emma Cow just stood there chewing her cud. She was happy. The rain kept the pesky flies off her back.

Sandy the Sow Pig giggled and wiggled in the first big mud puddle. "Oink Oink," giggle giggle, "Oink Oink," wiggle wiggle. She laughed and she oinked as she giggled and she wiggled.

Becky the Bunny ran into her favorite rabbit hole home. She did not want to get her new hat wet.

Becky the Bunny thanked God for the rain. Rain makes her carrots grow nice and juicy.

Tammy the Turtle was not afraid of the rain. She was nice and dry in her turtle shell home. Tammy the Turtle felt very special. She never has to run home. Her home is always with her.

Little Kicker noticed the rain had almost stopped.

The clouds began to go away. The happy birds and frogs started to sing.

Little Kicker learned that rain is important. Rain gives us water.

Little Kicker learned to pray when he is afraid.

The rain stopped and the sun came out.
A beautiful rainbow formed in the sky.

Tony the Pony came to play with Little Kicker.

Splash, splash, splash went the water as they ran across the field. They jumped over puddles and laughed and whinnied and hee hawed!

Little Kicker learned something about rain.
I wonder what it was.

Little Kicker learned to do something when he is afraid. I wonder what it was.

about Little Kicker Country

Plants and Animals of the Ozark Mountain Region

Fun facts and insights for adults to learn and teach to children about God's creation and provision

Page 6

Bullfrogs are native to much of North America. They grow quite large and make loud, deep, bass sounds in the evenings. Bullfrogs are aquatic and live around ponds and larger bodies of water. Daddy would sometimes bring Mother fresh frog legs for our supper. I always came to watch when Mother dropped them in a skillet of hot oil because the legs jumped all around the inside of the pan. They tasted just like chicken! Ha! Ha!

Meads Milkweed is a native plant to the Ozarks. It is a tall prairie grass, and because of loss of habitat, it is now on the endangered species list. I have often enjoyed its beauty.

Page 25

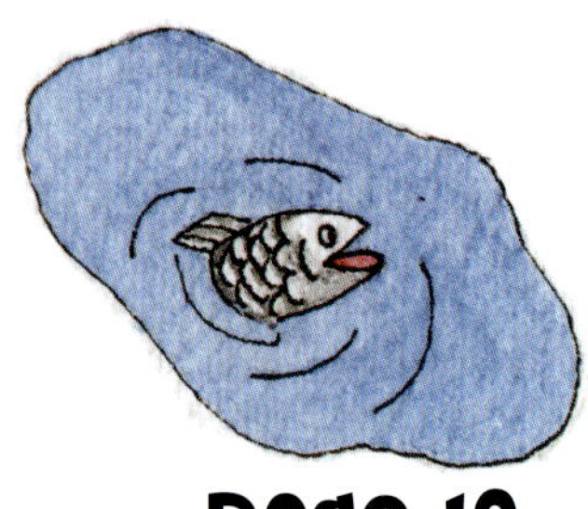

Page 16

Perch are delicious to eat and easy to catch. Just put a juicy red worm on your hook and wait for the action. My sister and I as children caught perch from the edge of Grandpa's pond. We decided to cook them as we had seen done in a western movie. We roasted them until they were tender. Everything was perfect ...until we bit into them and discovered we had forgotten to scale the fish. That ended our cooking experience on the gravel bank of Grandpa's pond.

Cardinals are beautiful, mild mannered songbirds. Seven states have chosen the cardinal as their state bird. Cardinals eat seeds and are native to North America. A legend is that early settlers named this bird after the Cardinals of the Catholic Church because its' bright, red feathers reminded them of the color of the Cardinal's robe.

Page 26

Fun Activities for Children

1. What does Mr. Frog say on page 6?
2. Count the raindrops in the water on pages 16 and 17.
3. Can you find A through N of the ABC's in the tree on page 17? (Hint: G, H, I and J are in the brown trunk of the tree.)
4. How many umbrellas are on pages 18 and 19?
5. What is Sandy the Sow Pig doing on page 23?
6. How many carrots are on page 24?
7. Can you find and name all of the animals on pages 28 and 29?

A Prayer For Little Kicker (Little Kicker is prayed for by family and friends.)

Little Kicker's First Rainstorm (Little Kicker is taught to pray to overcome his fears.)

Little Kicker Visits Doctor Quickwell (Little Kicker prays, and God sends an answer.)

Little Kicker Wants A Turn (Little Kicker faces rejection when he is not chosen to play with his friends, but Mother Donkey teaches Little Kicker that God has a plan.)

Coming soon!

Little Kicker Likes To Jump (Little Kicker plans his gigantic jump over Kimble Creek's watercress patch, causing Becky the Bunny to worry about her favorite snack.)

www.littlekicker.com

www.facebook.com/littlekickerbooks

Warning to parents and guardians of children: While most animals stay outside in rainstorms, if there is thunder, children should be indoors and away from windows. Even if thunder sounds distant, it may still be dangerous. Lightning can travel many miles from the thunder it produces. Military and civilian airports require ground personnel to take shelter if lightning is within five miles. We should do no less for our children.

God has great plans for children. In Psalm 127:3 God says children are a heritage from the Lord. Enjoy this gentle and uplifting story.